jesus + me

Illustration by Justin Hilden
Written by Sara Wade

About the Author:

Sara Wade graduated from Hamline University with a degree in theatre arts and elementary education. She spent some time teaching kindergarten in the public school system and worked with preschool children in a variety of settings before moving into her current role at Eagle Brook Church. In her role, Sara writes curriculum and teaches preschoolers in the Early Childhood program. Sara lives in Lino Lakes, Minn. with her husband and three young children.

NOTE FROM THE AUTHOR:
This book was designed and written as a guide to salvation in Jesus Christ. I whole-heartedly believe that preschool/kindergarten children can make a genuine decision to live for Jesus and will be saved if they choose to accept His forgiveness and grace. This book tells the amazing story of how Jesus willingly gave His life for us. I pray that your child will understand the incredible love that God has for him/her.

Tips for Sharing this Story:

- Find a time when you can focus your attention on your child and the message you are sharing.

- If your child is receptive and shows a desire to have Jesus as his/her leader, the last pages of this book will help you lead through that decision.

- Re-read this story often. It is a wonderful reminder of God's love and what Jesus did to save us.

About the Illustrator:

Justin Hilden is an illustrator and animation artist who has lived and worked in Los Angeles, Chicago, and St. Paul. He was a boy in the Wisconsin countryside, where he buried "treasures" made of wood and drew intricate maps to find them. The illustrations in this book were created using pencil, paper, and Photoshop. More examples of Justin's work may be viewed at **www.sluganimation.com**.

NOTE FROM THE ILLUSTRATOR:

- On each page you will see a dove which represents the Holy Spirit. The dove bridges the gap in time between the children and Jesus. You can also play a fun game with your child and find the dove on every page!

- In each picture of Jesus, you will see a red shawl. The shawl is interwoven through the images as a visual representation of His love and power.

Place your
child's photo
here

THiS BooK BELONGS to

• • • • • • • • • • • • • • • •

I made Jesus the Leader of my Life on

• • • • • • • • • • • • • • • •

Hello _____.
(child's name)

My name is God, the God of the whole world. I want to share a story with you. This is a story that I know you will love, because I wrote it. When I wrote this story I was thinking about you.

This story starts with

You _____ (child's name). Did you know that I made you? I made everyone. I gave you your _____ (eye color) eyes and _____ (hair color) hair. I chose _____ (birthdate) to be your birthday. I gave you a _____ (family member) and a _____ (family member) who love and care for you. I did all of these things for you because I love you very much.

_____ you are so special to me.
(child's name)
I love to watch you learn and play and grow. I see you when you share and show kindness. I see you when you follow directions. I am proud of you _____.
(child's name)

I know that sometimes it is hard to be good. Sometimes you make mistakes and do things that you shouldn't do. I call those things sin.

Sometimes when you sin you get in trouble and face consequences, don't you? Those consequences help you learn not to sin.

But, everybody in the whole world still makes mistakes and sins. One of the worst things that happens when you sin is that it keeps you from being close to me, God. Being away from me is the punishment for sin.

I want you to stay close to me _____. That
(child's name)
is why I sent my son, Jesus, to this earth for you.

Jesus was very special. He never, ever sinned. Jesus did amazing things and he helped a lot of people. Jesus had all the power of God, while he was on earth.

Most of all, Jesus showed people how to live the right way. Jesus showed love and kindness to everyone. _____, do you
(child's name)
know how to show love and kindness?

[Jesus made sick people better. Jesus made blind people see. Jesus stopped a storm. Jesus walked on water.]

I didn't send Jesus to the world just to show people how to live. Remember, I want to be close to you. So I made a plan for Jesus to take away the punishment for sin.

There were some men who didn't understand who Jesus was and decided to kill Him. Jesus felt afraid, but He knew it was all part of my plan. _____ have you ever felt
(child's name)
afraid? What did you do?

Even though Jesus was afraid, he loved you so much that he followed my plan. Jesus trusted me, God, to make things right in the world.

They put Jesus up high on a cross and left him there to die. When Jesus died on the cross, he took the punishment for your sins, so that you, and the rest of the world, wouldn't have to be punished.

After Jesus died, his body was put in a tomb and a big, heavy stone was put in front of it. Three days later, his friends came to the tomb and the stone was rolled away.

Jesus' body was gone. Jesus had risen from the dead. He came back to life!

_____ how do you think Jesus'
(child's name)
friends felt when they saw him alive again?

_____, I want you to know what this story
(child's name)

means for you. It means you can have

Jesus as the leader of your life.

If Jesus is your leader, I will forgive your sins.

With Jesus as your leader, you will follow Him

and He will help you make wise choices. He will

help you know what is right and wrong.

Sometimes you might still make mistakes and

there will still be consequences, but I will

always be there to forgive you.

One of the best things about having Jesus as the leader of your life is that someday you will get to live in heaven forever.

Heaven is a beautiful place with gold streets where there are no tears or hurting. Everyone there is kind and loving. Jesus and I will be with you in heaven. We have a special place there just for you, _____.
(child's name)

Hey Grown-Ups!

Is your child ready to accept Jesus as the Savior and Leader of his/her life?

How will you know?

Your Child:
- >> Can tell you that Jesus died to save him/her.
- >> Wants God's forgiveness.
- >> Asks you to pray with him/her.

What should you do?

1 Pray with your child.

You can have your child echo you line by line as you recite this special prayer with him/her.

> "For God loved the world so much that he gave his only Son. God gave his Son so that whoever believes in him may not be lost, but have eternal life."
> John 3:16

> Dear God, I love you. Thank you for loving me. I know I make mistakes that you call sin and my sin can keep me from being close to you. I want to be close to you forever. I believe Jesus loves me and died on the cross to save me. I know that you can forgive me because Jesus died. Please forgive me for my sins and let me stay close to you now, and forever in heaven. Jesus, You are my Savior and I want You to be the Leader of my Life. Amen.

2 Celebrate the wise decision your child made!

Remember all of heaven is celebrating too!

> "...there is joy before the angels of God when one sinner changes his heart."
> Luke 15:10

3 Continue to help and encourage your child to learn more and grow in Christ.

Here are some ways your child can grow in faith:
- Read the Bible with him/her
- Pray with and for him/her
- Talk about Jesus
- Bring him/her to church
- Encourage lots and lots of questions!

> "If you declare with your mouth, 'Jesus is Lord,' and if you believe in your heart that God raised Jesus from death, then you will be saved."
> Romans 10:9

> "But if we confess our sins, he will forgive our sins. We can trust God. He does what is right. He will make us clean from all the wrongs we have done."
> 1 John 1:9

COLORING PAGE